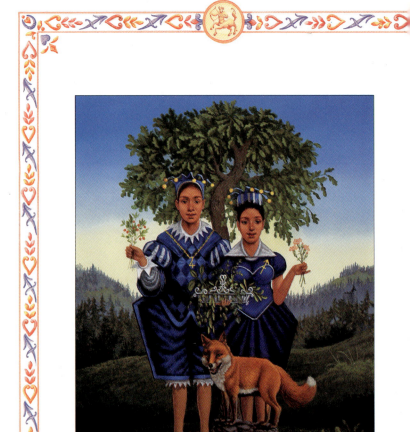

✶ L O V E S I G N S ✶

SAGITTARIUS

November 23 – December 21

JULIA & DEREK PARKER

DK

Dedicated to Martin Lethbridge

A D K P U B L I S H I N G B O O K

Project Editor • Annabel Morgan
Art Editor • Anna Benjamin
Managing Editor • Francis Ritter
Managing Art Editor • Derek Coombes
DTP Designer • Cressida Joyce
Production Controller • Martin Croshaw
US Editor • Constance M. Robinson

A C K N O W L E D G M E N T S

Photography: Steve Gorton: pp. 10, 13–15, 17–19, 46–49; Ian O'Leary: 16. *Additional photography by:* Colin Keates, David King, Monique Le Luhandre, David Murray, Tim Ridley, Clive Streeter, Harry Taylor, Matthew Ward. *Artworks:* Nic Demin: 34–45; Peter Lawman: *jacket,* 4, 12; Paul Redgrave: 24–33; Satwinder Sehmi: *glyphs;* Jane Thomson: *borders;* Rosemary Woods: 11.

Peter Lawman's paintings are exhibited by the Portal Gallery Ltd, London.

Picture credits: Bridgeman Art Library/Hermitage, St. Petersburg: 51; Robert Harding Picture Library: 20l, 20c, 20r; Images Colour Library: 9; The National Gallery, London: 11; Tony Stone Images: 21t, 21b; The Victoria and Albert Museum, London: 5; Zefa: 21c.

First American Edition, 1996
2 4 6 8 10 9 7 5 3 1

Published in the United States by
DK Publishing, Inc., 95 Madison Avenue, New York, New York 10016
Visit us on the World Wide Web at http://www.dk.com

A catalog record is available from the Library of Congress.

ISBN 0-7894-1097-4

Reproduced by Bright Arts, Hong Kong
Printed and bound by Imago, Hong Kong

CONTENTS

Astrology & You 8

Looking for a Lover 10

You & Your Lover 12

The Food of Love 16

Places to Love 20

Venus & Mars 22

Your Love Life 24

Your Sex Life 34

Tokens of Love 46

Your Permanent Relationship 50

Venus & Mars Tables 52

ASTROLOGY & YOU

THERE IS MUCH MORE TO ASTROLOGY THAN YOUR SUN SIGN.
A SIMPLE INVESTIGATION INTO THE POSITION OF THE OTHER
PLANETS AT THE MOMENT OF YOUR BIRTH WILL PROVIDE YOU
WITH FASCINATING INSIGHTS INTO YOUR PERSONALITY.

*Y*our birth sign, or Sun sign, is the sign of the zodiac that the Sun occupied at the moment of your birth. The majority of books on astrology concentrate only on explaining the relevance of the Sun signs. This is a simple form of astrology that can provide you with some interesting but rather general information about you and your personality. In this book, we take you a step further, and reveal how the planets Venus and Mars work in association with your Sun sign to influence your attitudes toward romance and sexuality.

In order to gain a detailed insight into your personality, a "natal" horoscope, or birth chart, is necessary. This details the position of all the planets in our solar system at the moment of your birth, not just the position of the Sun. Just as the Sun occupied one of the 12 zodiac signs when you were born, perhaps making you "a Geminian" or "a Sagittarian," so each of the other planets occupied a certain sign. Each planet governs a different area of your personality, and the planets Venus and Mars are responsible for your attitudes toward love and sex, respectively.

For example, if you are a Sun-sign Sagittarian, according to the attributes of the sign you should be a dynamic, freedom-loving character. However, if Venus occupied Libra when you were born, you may make a passive and clinging partner – qualities that are supposedly completely alien to Sagittarians.

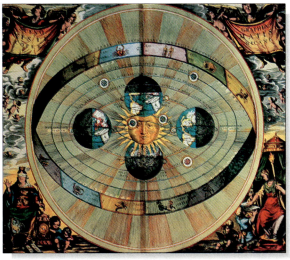

A MAP OF THE CONSTELLATION

The 16th-century astronomer Copernicus first made the revolutionary suggestion that the planets orbit the Sun rather than Earth. In this 17th-century constellation chart, the Sun is shown at the center of the solar system.

The tables on pages 52–61 of this book will enable you to discover the positions of Mars and Venus at the moment of your birth. Once you have read this information, turn to pages 22–45. On these pages we explain how the influences of Venus and Mars interact with the characteristics of your Sun sign. This information will provide you with many illuminating insights into your personality, and explains how the planets have formed your attitudes toward love and sex.

LOOKING FOR A LOVER

ASTROLOGY CAN PROVIDE YOU WITH VALUABLE INFORMATION
ON HOW TO INITIATE AND MAINTAIN RELATIONSHIPS. IT CAN
ALSO TELL YOU HOW COMPATIBLE YOU ARE WITH YOUR LOVER,
AND HOW SUCCESSFUL YOUR RELATIONSHIP IS LIKELY TO BE.

*P*eople frequently use astrology to lead into a relationship, and "What sign are you?" is often used as a conversation opener. Some people simply introduce the subject as an opening gambit, while others place great importance on this question and its answer.

Astrology can affect the way you think and behave when you are in love. It can also provide you with fascinating information about your lovers and your relationships. Astrology cannot tell you who to fall in love with or who to avoid, but it can offer you some very helpful advice.

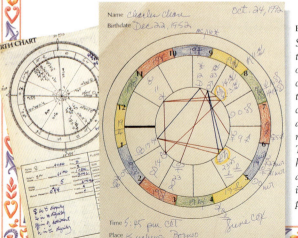

BIRTH CHARTS
Synastry involves the comparison of two people's charts in order to assess their compatibility in all areas of their relationship. The process can highlight any areas of common interest or potential conflict.

THE TABLE OF ELEMENTS

People whose signs are grouped under the same element tend to find it easy to fall into a happy relationship. The groupings are:

FIRE: *Aries, Leo, Sagittarius*
EARTH: *Taurus, Virgo, Capricorn*
AIR: *Gemini, Libra, Aquarius*
WATER: *Cancer, Scorpio, Pisces*

When you meet someone to whom you are attracted, astrology can provide you with a valuable insight into his or her personality. It may even reveal unattractive characteristics that your prospective partner is trying to conceal.

Astrologers are often asked to advise lovers involved in an ongoing relationship, or people who are contemplating a love affair. This important aspect of astrology is called synastry, and involves comparing the birth charts of the two people concerned. Each birth chart records the exact position of the planets at the moment and place of a person's birth.

By interpreting each chart separately, then comparing them, an astrologer can assess the compatibility of any two people, showing where problems may arise in their relationship, and where strong bonds will form.

One of the greatest astrological myths is that people of some signs are not compatible with people of certain other signs. This is completely untrue. Whatever your Sun sign, you can have a happy relationship with a person of any other sign.

YOU *&* YOUR LOVER

KNOWING ABOUT YOURSELF AND YOUR LOVER IS THE KEY TO
A HAPPY RELATIONSHIP. HERE WE REVEAL THE TRADITIONAL
ASSOCIATIONS OF SAGITTARIUS, YOUR COMPATIBILITY WITH ALL
THE SUN SIGNS, AND THE FLOWERS LINKED WITH EACH SIGN.

THE OAK TREE IS
TRADITIONALLY
ASSOCIATED
WITH
SAGITTARIUS

RICH ROYAL BLUE
AND DEEP
DRAMATIC
PURPLE
ARE THE
SAGITTARIAN
COLORS

JUPITER RULES
OVER THE
SIGN OF
SAGITTARIUS

SAGE IS
ONE OF THE
MANY HERBS
ATTRIBUTED
TO THIS SIGN

SAGITTARIANS
OFTEN HAVE
THICKSET AND
MUSCULAR
BODIES, WITH
STURDY LEGS

ALL ANIMALS
RELATED TO THE
HUNT, INCLUDING
THE FOX, ARE
GOVERNED BY
SAGITTARIUS

SAGITTARIUS AND ARIES
Sagittarius and Aries are both dynamic fire signs, and the active Arien sex drive will match your powerful libido. You both need freedom, so your relationship may lack a real sense of commitment.

Lavender is a Geminian flower

Thistles are ruled by Aries

SAGITTARIUS AND GEMINI
You have similar personalities – both witty, restless, and sociable. As a result, you will be good companions as well as lovers, and this pairing could come close to being the perfect match.

SAGITTARIUS AND TAURUS
Steady Taureans are cautious, and may be slow to respond to your boisterous overtures, but you will be swept away by their ardor and passion once your relationship is established.

The lily, and other white flowers, are ruled by Cancer

The rose is associated with Taurus

SAGITTARIUS AND CANCER
This is not an easy combination of signs. The Cancerian love of domesticity has little in common with your love of freedom, but a strong mutual attraction can make this partnership succeed.

SAGITTARIUS AND LEO

Optimistic and high-spirited Sagittarians are a perfect match for bold and adventurous Leos. This is potentially one of the most colorful and rewarding combinations in the zodiac.

Hydrangeas are governed by Libra

Sunflowers are ruled by Leo

SAGITTARIUS AND LIBRA

This could be an extremely happy and harmonious pairing. Libran tact and diplomacy will temper your blunt and outspoken Sagittarian ways, and you will boost low Libran energy levels.

SAGITTARIUS AND VIRGO

Virgos and Sagittarians make a good match. Self-sufficient and sensible Virgos will give you plenty of freedom, and you will charm them with your Sagittarian exuberance and high spirits.

Honeysuckle is attributed to Scorpio

Small, brightly colored flowers are associated with Virgo

SAGITTARIUS AND SCORPIO

You will be taken aback by the intensity of Scorpio passion, and Scorpio may find your honesty and optimism brash and naive. An energetic and exciting sex life can hold you together.

SAGITTARIUS AND SAGITTARIUS
Two Sagittarians are guaranteed to have a lively and vivacious relationship. Try to overcome your yearning for freedom and adventure, or you may both end up in hot pursuit of other prey.

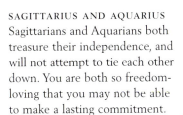

Orchids are associated with Aquarius

Carnations are ruled by Sagittarius

SAGITTARIUS AND AQUARIUS
Sagittarians and Aquarians both treasure their independence, and will not attempt to tie each other down. You are both so freedom-loving that you may not be able to make a lasting commitment.

SAGITTARIUS AND CAPRICORN
A Capricorn will bring you down to earth and make you a little more practical. In return, you will bring fun, excitement, and entertainment to a serious-minded Capricorn.

Viburnum is governed by Pisces

Pansies are Capricorn flowers

SAGITTARIUS AND PISCES
You will take the excesses of Piscean emotion in your stride, and Pisceans will be cheered by your lighthearted outlook on life. This is a very well-matched fire and water combination.

THE FOOD OF LOVE

WHEN PLANNING A SEDUCTION, THE SENSUOUS DELIGHTS OF AN
EXQUISITE MEAL SHOULD NEVER BE UNDERESTIMATED. READ ON
TO DISCOVER THE PERFECT MEAL FOR EACH OF THE SUN SIGNS,
GUARANTEED TO AROUSE INTEREST AND STIR DESIRE.

*Sagittarians
will find
nutty onion
flan delicious,
because onions
are traditionally
associated with
this sign.*

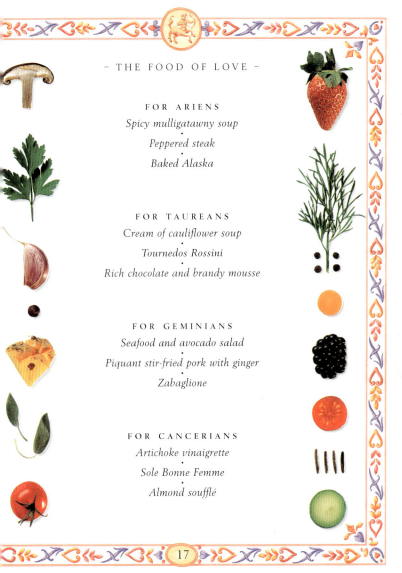

- THE FOOD OF LOVE -

FOR ARIENS
Spicy mulligatawny soup
·
Peppered steak
·
Baked Alaska

FOR TAUREANS
Cream of cauliflower soup
·
Tournedos Rossini
·
Rich chocolate and brandy mousse

FOR GEMINIANS
Seafood and avocado salad
·
Piquant stir-fried pork with ginger
·
Zabaglione

FOR CANCERIANS
Artichoke vinaigrette
·
Sole Bonne Femme
·
Almond soufflé

– THE FOOD OF LOVE –

FOR LEOS

Roasted tomato and garlic soup

·

Boeuf Stroganoff

·

Pears cooked in wine

FOR VIRGOS

Eggplant salad

·

Paella

·

French apple tart

FOR LIBRANS

Asparagus with hollandaise sauce

·

Pork with roasted apples

·

Strawberry Pavlova

FOR SCORPIOS

Vichyssoise

·

Lobster Newburg

·

Blueberry cream

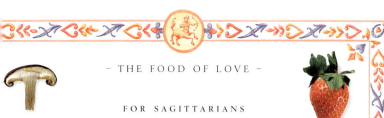

- THE FOOD OF LOVE -

FOR SAGITTARIANS

Chilled cucumber soup

·

Nutty onion flan

·

Rhubarb crumble with fresh cream

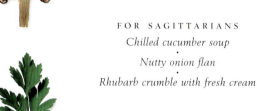

FOR CAPRICORNS

Eggs Florentine

·

Pork tenderloin stuffed with sage

·

Pineapple Pavlova

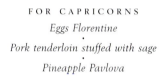

FOR AQUARIANS

Watercress soup

·

Chicken cooked with chili and lime

·

Lemon soufflé

FOR PISCEANS

French onion soup

·

Trout au vin rosé

·

Melon sorbet

PLACES TO LOVE

ONCE YOU HAVE WON YOUR LOVER'S HEART, A ROMANTIC VACATION TOGETHER WILL SEAL YOUR LOVE. HERE, YOU CAN DISCOVER THE PERFECT DESTINATION FOR EACH SUN SIGN, FROM HISTORIC CITIES TO IDYLLIC BEACHES.

THE EIFFEL TOWER, PARIS

ARIES

Florence is an Arien city, and its perfectly preserved Renaissance palaces and churches will set the scene for wonderful romance.

TAURUS

The unspoiled scenery and unhurried pace of life in rural Ireland is sure to appeal to patient and placid Taureans.

GEMINI

Vivacious and restless Geminians will feel at home in the fast-paced and sophisticated atmosphere of New York.

CANCER

The watery beauty and uniquely romantic atmosphere of Venice is guaranteed to arouse passion and stir the Cancerian imagination.

ST. BASIL'S CATHEDRAL, MOSCOW

AYERS ROCK/ULURU, AUSTRALIA

THE PYRAMIDS,
EGYPT

GONDOLAS,
VENICE

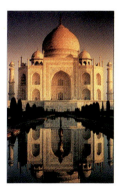

THE TAJ MAHAL,
INDIA

LEO

*Leos will fall in love
all over again when
surrounded by the
picturesque charm and
unspoiled medieval
atmosphere of Prague.*

VIRGO

*Perhaps the most
elegant and romantic
of all cities, Paris is
certainly the ideal
setting for a stylish and
fastidious Virgo.*

LIBRA

*The dramatic and
exotic beauty of Upper
Egypt and the Nile will
provide the perfect
backdrop for wooing
a romantic Libran.*

SCORPIO

*Intense and passionate
Scorpios will be strongly
attracted by the whiff
of danger present in
the exotic atmosphere
of New Orleans.*

SAGITTARIUS

*The wide-ranging
spaces of the Australian
outback will appeal
to the Sagittarian love
of freedom and the
great outdoors.*

CAPRICORN

*Capricorns will be
fascinated and inspired
by the great historical
monuments of Moscow,
the most powerful of all
Russian cities.*

AQUARIUS

*Intrepid Aquarians will
be enthralled and
amazed by the unusual
sights and spectacular
landscapes of the
Indian subcontinent.*

PISCES

*Water-loving Pisceans
will be at their most
relaxed and romantic
by the sea, perhaps on
a small and unspoiled
Mediterranean island.*

VENUS & MARS

LUCID, SHINING VENUS AND FIERY, RED MARS HAVE ALWAYS BEEN
ASSOCIATED WITH HUMAN LOVE AND PASSION. THE TWO
PLANETS HAVE A POWERFUL INFLUENCE ON OUR ATTITUDES
TOWARD LOVE, SEX, AND RELATIONSHIPS.

*T*he study of astrology first began long before humankind began to record its own history. The earliest astrological artifacts discovered, scratches on bones recording the phases of the Moon, date from well before the invention of any alphabet or writing system.

The planets Venus and Mars have always been regarded as having enormous significance in astrology. This is evident from the tentative attempts of early astrologers to record the effects of the two planets on humankind. Hundreds of years later, the positions of the planets were carefully noted in personal horoscopes. The earliest known record is dated 410 BC: "Venus [was] in the Bull, and Mars in the Twins."

The bright, shining planet Venus represents the gentle effect of the soul on our physical lives. It is responsible for a refined and romantic sensuality – "pure" love, untainted by sex. Venus reigns over our attitudes toward romance and the spiritual dimension of love.

The planet Mars affects the physical aspects of our lives – our strength, both physical and mental; our endurance; and our ability to fight for survival. Mars is also strongly linked to the sex drive of both men and women. Mars governs our physical energy, sexuality, and levels of desire.

Venus is known as an "inferior" planet, because its orbit falls between Earth and the Sun. Venus orbits the Sun

LOVE CONQUERS ALL

In Botticelli's Venus and Mars, *the warlike, fiery
energy of Mars, the god of war, has been overcome by
the gentle charms of Venus, the goddess of love.*

closely, and its position in the zodiac is always in a sign near that of the Sun. As a result, the planet can only have occupied one of five given signs at the time of your birth – your Sun sign, or the two signs before or after it. For example, if you were born with the Sun in Virgo, Venus can only have occupied Cancer, Leo, Virgo, Libra, or Scorpio at that moment.

Mars, on the other hand, is a "superior" planet. Its orbit lies on the other side of Earth from the Sun, and therefore the planet may have occupied any of the 12 signs at the moment of your birth.

On the following pages (24–45) we provide you with fascinating insights into how Mars and Venus govern your attitudes toward love, sex, and relationships. To ascertain which sign of the zodiac the planets occupied at the moment of your birth, you must first consult the tables on pages 52–61. Then turn to page 24 and read on.

YOUR LOVE LIFE

THE PLANET VENUS REPRESENTS LOVE, HARMONY, AND UNITY. WORK OUT WHICH SIGN OF THE ZODIAC VENUS OCCUPIED AT THE MOMENT OF YOUR BIRTH (SEE PAGES 52–57), AND READ ON.

VENUS IN LIBRA

When Venus shines from Libra, the planet will impart a gentle sense of romance and diplomacy to your forceful and exuberant Sagittarian personality. As a result you will be a sympathetic, tender, and understanding lover, with an abundance of seductive charm.

Your desire to form a secure long-term relationship will be increased by this position of Venus, because the influence of Libra creates a strong need for a secure and stable partnership. Once you have settled into a permanent alliance, you will not be plagued by the longing for freedom suffered by so many Sagittarians. You will be an affectionate, dependent and demonstrative partner, and

should be able to enjoy your relationship without feeling confined or tied down.

Sagittarians thrive on the thrill and drama of the chase. Having succeeded in seducing their lover, they can quickly lose interest, and turn to infidelity to provide a little novelty and excitement. Fortunately, when Venus shines from Libra, your yearning for a permanent relationship will make you a reliable and trustworthy lover, and you are unlikely to become involved in illicit liaisons.

Although the influence of Venus from Libra will not transform you into a starry-eyed romantic, your whole attitude toward love is likely to be more generous and sympathetic than

that of other Sagittarians. The slightly brash and insensitive elements of your personality will be toned down by tactful Libra, and you will be a diplomatic and understanding friend and lover.

Harmonious relationships are important to you – you dislike disagreements and confrontations. You may be so eager to please that you always take the line of least resistance, agreeing with everything your lover says.

However, you must not become ingratiating in your attempts to keep your lover happy.

This planetary placing will make you contented, good-tempered, and relaxed, and you will be surrounded by a wide circle of friends. The dynamism and warmheartedness of Sagittarius will be softened by the gentleness and romance of Libra, and you will be a loving and considerate partner.

VENUS IN SCORPIO

*T*he fiery, lively energy of Sagittarius will be heightened by this placing of Venus, because the planet is dynamic and vigorous when it shines from powerful Scorpio.

Of all the signs of the zodiac, Scorpio is perhaps the most sexual, forceful, and passionate. When Venus occupies this sign, your sexuality will be heightened, and you will need a partner with a similarly high sex drive. However, you will also demand an intellectual dimension to your romance, and will only be truly happy in a relationship that offers both sexual fulfillment and mental stimulation.

You may find that your Sagittarian longing for freedom and independence clashes with the depth of feeling and intensity of emotion that Venus brings from Scorpio. Sagittarius is essentially an uncomplicated, lighthearted sign, and you may be almost frightened by the intensity and power of your underlying emotions. While Scorpio is motivated by a desire to form a serious relationship, the Sagittarian need for freedom and independence is likely to continually assert itself, causing you some confusion. You may also find that Scorpio brings a jealous streak to your personality. This is a quality that your trusting and honest Sagittarian nature will loathe and detest. However, if you are able to adopt a determinedly rational and philosophical approach to this problem, you should be able to fight off any pangs of jealousy without too much difficulty.

Although you are among the sexiest and most libidinous of Sagittarians, you also possess a strong romantic streak, and will devote much energy to organizing memorable outings and special occasions for you and your lover.

These will vary from adventurous expeditions to an intimate meal with an expensive bottle of wine. Needless to say, your lover will be thrilled and flattered by your romantic attentions.

Sagittarius tends to be an extremely candid and forthright sign, but when Venus shines from Scorpio, you may be more secretive than your fellow Sagittarians. You will be quieter, more passionate, and more intense, and your partner must not underestimate the depth and complexity of your emotions.

The intensity of Scorpio will add passion and integrity to the lighthearted optimism of Sagittarius. If you can control your powerful emotions, and adopt a philosophical attitude toward your relationship, you will make a devoted, energetic, and warmhearted partner, with no shortage of admirers.

VENUS IN SAGITTARIUS

*P*eople born with both the Sun and Venus in Sagittarius will find all their personality traits are emphasized by this planetary placing. You are likely to be a gregarious, warmhearted, and enthusiastic lover, and will thrive in lively and sociable surroundings.

Good company and a light-hearted, cheerful atmosphere are important to you. Because you are such fun to be with, you are likely to have a long line of admirers competing for your attention. However, Sagittarius is a freedom-loving and independent sign, and the concept of tying yourself down to one person is unlikely to appeal. Not only do you dread the loss of your independence, but you are also easily bored, constantly seeking excitement and novelty. The concept of a staid and settled existence is not your ideal, and although

it may be easy for a romantic Sagittarian to fall in love, it will be more difficult for you to make a permanent commitment.

Sagittarians are the hunters of the zodiac, and they revel in the excitement of the chase. Even if you become happily ensconced in a permanent relationship, you may find it hard to prevent yourself from pursuing someone you find attractive. The dangerous thrill of infidelity will stimulate you, and you may even find yourself becoming involved in two or more affairs at the same time. These passing affairs may briefly entertain and amuse you, but in order to attain true fulfillment you will have to find one partner and settle down.

Although Venus in Sagittarius will bring you plenty of stamina and a powerful sex drive, you will also want to enjoy a mental rapport with your partner.

Stimulating discussion and debate must play a considerable part in your relationship if it is to hold your interest.

Sagittarians tend to be good-natured and easygoing partners. You will want your relationship to be fun, and may turn tail and flee if your lover adopts an over-intense or serious attitude. You cannot bear to feel restricted or confined. Your lover must appreciate this and allow you a measure of independence if your relationship is to be successful. You will not tolerate a jealous or possessive partner for very long.

Sagittarius has a broad romantic streak, and you will revel in the drama and excitement of being in love. If you can overcome your fear of commitment and resist the temptation of infidelity, you will be an exhilaratingly inventive, energetic, and original partner.

VENUS IN CAPRICORN

*W*hen Venus shines from Capricorn, the planet will calm the boisterous energy of Sagittarius and will encourage you to take your relationship more seriously than many of your carefree fellow Sagittarians.

The dignity and formality of Capricorn may suppress your Sagittarian exuberance and enthusiasm. Although you can appear a little cool and distant, in truth you are a tremendously kindhearted, supportive, and loyal lover. Due to this placing, you may be embarrassed by overt displays of emotion, but you must not conceal your innate warmth of heart and zest for life, because these qualities will attract a swarm of admirers.

This planetary placing will bring you a more sober attitude toward your love life. You will be a thoughtful, constant, and supportive partner, and once you have made a commitment,

you will want to remain faithful. Due to the disciplined influence of Capricorn, you will dislike flightiness and unreliability, and in theory infidelity will hold no appeal for you. However, Sagittarian duality may not be entirely quashed by Capricorn, and you are likely to suffer an occasional urge to indulge in a thrilling illicit liaison. Luckily, these urges should be suppressed by the conventionality and caution typical of Capricorn.

When you fall in love, you will be an extremely caring and devoted partner. However, you will retain your Sagittarian love of freedom and will be repelled by any manifestation of jealousy or possessiveness on the part of your lover.

When Venus shines from Capricorn, material status and wealth will be important to you. You are likely to be very conscious of status, and will

work hard to achieve a high standard of living and all the trappings of wealth and success. You may try to improve your status or win the admiration of others by choosing a lover who is particularly attractive, wealthy, or successful. Selecting a partner for such superficial reasons will not provide a stable base on which to build a relationship. Therefore, you must choose a partner for the right reasons.

From Capricorn, Venus will bring you many valuable and helpful qualities. You will be sensible, hardworking, and remarkably practical. However, do not allow the powerful influence of Venus to repress the warmth, spontaneity, and exuberance of your Sagittarian Sun sign. Combine the best of both signs, and you will make a reliable, loving, and extremely entertaining partner.

VENUS IN AQUARIUS

*W*hen Venus shines from Aquarius on a Sun-sign Sagittarian, the planet will have two main effects. First, Venus will increase your powerful need for independence, and second, it will cool the ardent and fiery passions of Sagittarius.

The calming effect of Venus can only be beneficial, for the active, energetic, and exuberant nature of Sagittarius needs no additional emphasis. This placing will make you more thoughtful and reflective. You are likely to pause for thought before flinging yourself impetuously into a love affair, and will think twice before making rash promises you will not be able to keep.

Although the dispassionate influence of Venus in Aquarius may prove valuable, the increased need for independence brought by Venus may not be quite so helpful. Beneath the boisterous enthusiasm of a Sun-sign Sagittarian, you are likely to be an intensely private person, and the prospect of sacrificing your independence will terrify you. Despite your friendly and gregarious demeanor, you may be wary of forming a permanent emotional relationship, simply because you are so reluctant to relinquish your much-treasured freedom and independence.

You must employ all the warmth and enthusiasm of your Sun sign to help you overcome your fear of commitment. If you are able to find a lively and intelligent lover who is happy to allow you a large measure of freedom, you will be extremely content.

Once you have found your soul mate, you will find it far easier to be faithful than most other Sagittarians. Infidelity is unlikely to tempt you, for Aquarius is an extremely loyal and constant sign.

Although you tend to have an introverted air of detachment, you will be a very sociable and supportive friend. You are likely to enjoy many close friendships, because such relationships do not threaten your independence in the same way as a long-term romantic alliance.

From Aquarius, Venus often brings an air of indefinable allure and glamor. You are not likely to suffer from a lack of potential partners – indeed, you may have to fend off a veritable throng of admirers. Aquarius is an original and idiosyncratic sign, and this placing may make you slightly eccentric. You are likely to embrace unconventionality, and may go out of your way to shock. This is also a Sagittarian trait, but do not give it free rein – your nonconformity may begin to embarrass people rather than entertain them.

YOUR SEX LIFE

THE PLANET MARS REPRESENTS PHYSICAL AND SEXUAL ENERGY.
WORK OUT WHICH SIGN OF THE ZODIAC MARS OCCUPIED AT THE
MOMENT OF YOUR BIRTH (SEE PAGES 58–61), AND READ ON.

MARS IN ARIES

The powerful energy and assertiveness of Mars in Aries will invigorate your lively Sagittarian sexuality, and you must make sure that you find a satisfying outlet for your abundance of sexual energy.

You are an ardent lover, and revel in the pursuit of a potential partner. However, Sagittarius is a restless sign, and Mars can bring a selfish streak from Aries. Once you have won your lover's heart, you may tire of him or her and look around for new prey.

Both Sagittarius and Aries are fire signs, and you are likely to have a hot temper. Try not to flare up too easily – you may appear aggressive and abrasive.

MARS IN TAURUS

From Taurus, Mars will boost your powerful Sagittarian sex drive. The Taurean influence will also help you to slow down and will encourage you to take your time when it comes to lovemaking. As a result, you will be a sensual, eager, and energetic lover with a considerable sexual appetite and an uncomplicated attitude towards your sexuality.

Mars in Taurus will bring tenacity and determination, and Sagittarius revels in the chase.

Consequently, when you set your sights on someone who plays hard to get, you will be spurred into a determined pursuit, and you will not give up until you have seduced the object of your affections.

Taurean patience will steady your boisterous nature, but from Taurus, Mars is capable of provoking sudden outbursts of rage. Make sure that your anger is not too strongly expressed, because you can be intimidating in the heat of an argument.

MARS IN GEMINI

*B*oth Sagittarius and Gemini are flirtatious signs, and you are likely to leave a trail of broken hearts behind you wherever you go. You regard lovemaking as a delightful diversion, and are a very light-hearted lover. Intensity and dark passion do not appeal – for you, sex should be entertaining, energetic, and adventurous.

The combination of Mars in Gemini with Sagittarius will not encourage fidelity. This placing is likely to tempt you to be unfaithful to your lover, and you may not be able to resist the thrill of a forbidden liaison.

When Mars shines from Gemini, your Sagittarian restlessness will be increased. Any monotony or routine will soon bore and irritate you, and a lively mind and sharp sense of humor will interest you more than good looks or a sexy body. Only an exciting and challenging mental rapport with your lover will guarantee a successful and long-lasting relationship.

MARS IN CANCER

*W*hen Mars shines from Cancer, your emotional energy may be stronger than your physical energy. However, once your interest and appetite have been aroused, you will be a sensual and responsive lover.

Despite the Sagittarian love of freedom and independence, a powerful longing for emotional security motivates all those born with Mars in Cancer. For you, sexual contact with your lover is a means of reassuring you that you are loved and wanted. Only when you feel totally secure and protected will you have the confidence to reveal yourself as a powerful and passionate lover.

Although many Sagittarians are excited by the thought of infidelity, illicit affairs are not likely to appeal to you. Due to the influence of Cancer, your long-term relationship will be the central focus of your existence, and you will not be prepared to sacrifice it just for a brief fling. You will demand total fidelity from yourself and your lover.

MARS IN LEO

Sagittarians are ardent and warmhearted lovers, and when Mars shines from Leo, the planet will bring you even more energy and enthusiasm. Your lovemaking will be passionate and hot-blooded, and you will possess plenty of stamina.

Mars in Leo is likely to imbue you with a larger-than-life glamor and magnetism, and you will have no shortage of admirers. You are a true hedonist, and sex will be one of your greatest pleasures. It is important to you that your affairs take place in the most elegant and luxurious surroundings possible. The thought of making love in unexpected and possibly uncomfortable surroundings will not excite you – you will want your seductions to take place in a suitably romantic atmosphere.

The duality of Sagittarius is likely to be suppressed by the devoted faithfulness of Leo. Illicit affairs will not appeal, and you will also demand unswerving fidelity from your partner.

MARS IN VIRGO

The cool restraint of Mars in Virgo should greatly benefit a bold, exuberant, and impetuous Sagittarian. You will be more sensitive and tactful than your fellow Sagittarians, and will be a more thoughtful, considerate, and gentle lover.

From Virgo, Mars will easily check any Sagittarian tendency toward infidelity. Virgo is an intensely loyal and constant sign. This planetary placing will help you to battle against the temptation to indulge in more than one affair at the same time, or to become enmeshed in a long string of illicit affairs.

When Mars occupies Virgo, the planet can bring a tendency to be difficult and critical. However, the cheerful, optimistic nature of Sagittarius should quell any Virgoan discontent.

When the earthy sensuality of practical, modest Virgo is harnessed to the lighthearted enthusiasm of Sagittarius, you will make a delightfully warm and honest lover.

MARS IN LIBRA

The powerful energy of Mars is always slightly lessened when the planet occupies Libra. As a result, you will possess a tranquil and equable nature, and may find that due to the languid influence of Libra, sex sometimes seems a little too exhausting and strenous. This is very out of character for a dynamic and hot-blooded Sagittarian. Therefore, you must try and use the energy and exuberance of your Sun sign to give your libido a boost.

However, a persevering potential partner may be lucky enough to discover that your sensuality is actually heightened by this placing, and that once you are aroused, you will respond with surprising eagerness and passion.

Sagittarius tends toward duality, and Libra is very easily led. Consequently, this placing may encourage you to drift into infidelity. You must resolve to be faithful, because an illicit affair may ruin a happy and rewarding long-term relationship.

MARS IN SCORPIO

*W*hen the sexual energy of Scorpio is combined with the fiery assertiveness of Mars and added to a dynamic and adventurous Sagittarian personality, sparks may fly.

From this sign, Mars will bring you additional sexual vigor and a strong appetite for sex. It is essential that you find satisfying and frequent sexual fulfillment. Due to the duality of Sagittarius you may feel that this will be best achieved with several different partners.

However, you may experience some conflict between your deep-seated Scorpio desire for commitment and your strong Sagittarian urge to play the field. You might become discontented and dissatisfied with fleeting affairs, and long to settle down with one partner. If you are able to find a lover with an equally high sex drive and an energetic and enthusiastic outlook on life, you should be able to form a contented, fulfilling, and loving permanent alliance.

MARS IN SAGITTARIUS

*W*hen both Mars and the Sun occupy Sagittarius, all the qualities of the sign are emphasized. You will have a great abundance of physical energy, and the ability to express your love warmly, affectionately, and wholeheartedly to your partner.

This placing may encourage the Sagittarian tendency toward unconventionality. You may try to shock people in order to enjoy their outraged reactions. Your eccentricity can be very amusing and appealing, but do not allow it to get out of hand, because it may become more embarrassing than entertaining.

Sagittarius is the hunter of the zodiac, and you may regard everyone as prospective prey. You will revel in the excitement of the chase, but once you have trapped your quarry, you may lose interest. A succession of brief affairs will not bring you lasting fulfillment, so do not allow your restlessness to prevent you from forming a happy, long-lasting relationship.

MARS IN CAPRICORN

*F*rom Capricorn, Mars will make you extremely ambitious and competitive, eager to excel in every area, including sex and seduction. Your love-making will be skillful and sensual, and your lover will enjoy your vigor and expertise.

Your forceful charm and determination is guaranteed to bowl over any potential lover. However, once you settle down in a permanent relationship, your partner may find that not quite so much of your time and attention is available. Once you have won your lover's heart, the challenge has gone, and you may lose interest. You may even choose to become absorbed in your Capricorn ambitions and your Sagittarian flirtations.

Try not to neglect your lover. In order to achieve a happy and rewarding relationship, you must direct some of your formidable energies toward keeping your partner happy. This should not be difficult, for when you try, you are charming and witty.

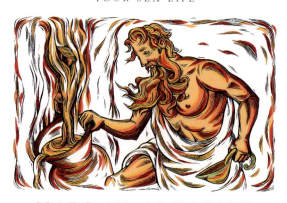

MARS IN AQUARIUS

From Aquarius, Mars may increase your Sagittarian reluctance to settle down and sacrifice your independence. Although you will enjoy sex, and are an adventurous and exciting lover, your deep-seated fear of losing your freedom may hold you back from forming a long-term emotional relationship. Indeed, you may realize that your lover is much more eager than you are to put things on a more serious footing and to make a lasting commitment.

Sagittarius is a freethinking and nonconformist sign, and this placing will enhance your unconventionality. Your originality and unpredictability are likely to delight your partner. Your sex life should be inventive and imaginative, and you will be eager to experiment.

Aquarius is an intensely loyal and honorable sign, and once committed, you will take your relationship very seriously. This placing should control any hint of Sagittarian duality.

MARS IN PISCES

*T*he influence of Mars in Pisces will emphasize your sensuality and passion, and raise your emotional level considerably. Your lovemaking will combine the energy and ardor of fiery Sagittarius with the sensitivity and tenderness of watery Pisces. As a result, you may leave your lovers quite weak at the knees with desire.

Mars in Pisces may bring you a tendency toward secretiveness and deceit. If these qualities combine with Sagittarian duality, you may be tempted by the forbidden thrill of clandestine affairs and dangerous liaisons.

Although Sagittarius is an open and forthright sign, Pisces does not find it easy to face up to problems. This placing may encourage you to deal with any difficulties in your relationship by pretending that they do not exist. This approach will not help to solve your problems, so enlist the help of forthright Sagittarius and tackle your problems boldly and bravely.

TOKENS OF LOVE

ASTROLOGY CAN GIVE YOU A FASCINATING INSIGHT INTO YOUR LOVER'S PERSONALITY AND ATTITUDE TOWARD LOVE. IT CAN ALSO PROVIDE YOU WITH SOME INVALUABLE HINTS WHEN YOU WANT TO CHOOSE THE PERFECT GIFT FOR YOUR LOVER.

JEWELED
HAIR CLIP

GOLD
PADLOCK
BRACELET

SILKY
SCARF

ARIES
Ariens will adore a bold, brightly colored scarf. Hair accessories will also make an ideal gift.

ITALIAN
BOTTLE
OPENER

TAURUS
Taureans love wine and are discriminating connoisseurs; therefore, any wine-related gifts will bring great pleasure.

GEMINI
Geminians love jewelry, especially bracelets and rings. A handsome box of mixed nuts or Jordan almonds will also be greatly appreciated by a Geminian.

CANCER

Cancerians adore unusual curios and antiques, especially silver.

HEART-SHAPED
SILVER TRINKET
BOX

ANTIQUE INDIAN
PERFUME BOTTLE

ORIGINAL OIL
PAINTING

CRYSTALLIZED
FRUITS

LEO

A bottle of expensive perfume will appeal to a sensual Leo. An original painting is equally likely to please.

VIRGO

Instead of chocolates, give your health-conscious Virgoan lover a box of crystallized fruits or a jar of exotic honey.

– TOKENS OF LOVE –

LIBRA

Librans are true romantics and will be thrilled by a recording of their favorite classical music, or a video of a sentimental old film.

DECORATIVE
TOOTHBRUSH

SCORPIO

Scorpios will be delighted by an attractive leather belt or wallet. Decorative bathroom accessories will also please your Scorpio lover because Scorpio is a water sign.

PATTERNED
LEATHER BELT

SAGITTARIUS

Adventurous and independent Sagittarians love to travel all over the globe. Any travel books or accessories, such as maps or compasses, will be appreciated by your Sagittarian lover.

VICTORIAN
TRAVEL BOOKS

VIOLIN

ENAMELED
GLOBE PILLBOX

– TOKENS OF LOVE –

OLD-FASHIONED
FOUNTAIN PEN

CAPRICORN

Only the best will
do for a fastidious
Capricorn. A
fine fountain pen
or an antique silver
picture frame is sure
to impress your
Capricorn lover.

GIVING A BIRTHSTONE

*The most personal
gift you can give
your lover is the
gem linked to his
or her Sun sign.*

TOPAZ

ARIES: *diamond*
TAURUS: *emerald*
GEMINI: *agate* • CANCER: *pearl*
LEO: *ruby* • VIRGO: *sardonyx*
LIBRA: *sapphire* • SCORPIO: *opal*
SAGITTARIUS: *topaz*
CAPRICORN: *amethyst*
AQUARIUS: *aquamarine*
PISCES: *moonstone*

AQUARIUS

Unusual hand-
thrown modern
pottery will please
an Aquarian lover.
If you are giving
flowers, choose
orchids.

HAND-
THROWN
POTTERY
MUG

IRIDESCENT
GLASS
MARBLES

PISCES

*Iridescent glassware
is guaranteed to
delight your
Piscean lover.*

WHITE
ORCHIDS

YOUR PERMANENT
RELATIONSHIP

IF YOU CAN OVERCOME THE TYPICAL SAGITTARIAN FEAR
OF RESTRICTION AND CONFINEMENT, YOU WILL MAKE AN
ENCOURAGING, STIMULATING, AND OPTIMISTIC PARTNER.

Sagittarians will not tolerate a relationship that is in any way restrictive or claustrophobic. You need to feel free, and a partner who wants to rule your life or confine you too closely will be going about things in exactly the wrong way.

You cannot endure jealousy and will be greatly upset by any manifestation of this emotion from your lover. Your roving Sagittarian eye may sometimes give your partner reason to be jealous, but a wise mate will avoid acting on those feelings. However, once you have committed yourself to a partner you love and with whom you want to spend the rest of your life, it will do you no harm to restrain that roving eye.

You thrive on challenge, and one way of satisfying your yearning for constant stimulation is to choose a lover who will continually intrigue and surprise you. "Never a dull moment" is the ideal Sagittarian motto, and life with a partner who is not ready and willing to share in adventure will never be entirely satisfactory.

You are a passionate lover, able to express your love warmly and rewardingly. Although sexual compatibility is important, you need shared interests outside the bedroom. You and your partner should also be on the same intellectual wavelength – while healthy competition should exist between you, one must never entirely outstrip the other.

On a Sailing Ship, *by Caspar David Friedrich, shows a newly married couple sailing into a bright but unknown future together.*

The Sagittarian who pants along in the wake of a more brilliant lover may find the situation a little difficult to cope with.

Anyone involved in a relationship with a Sagittarian must occasionally wonder whether that partner is taking the relationship quite seriously enough. You have a rather flippant attitude toward love; even when you feel most deeply you find it hard to express your feelings. Try to make the effort, for your partner will yearn for reassurance of your love at times.

Sagittarians make wonderful parents, since children respond well to their energy, enthusiasm, and joy in living. However, you will still need some time of your own in order to prevent yourself from feeling too tied down and confined.

VENUS & MARS TABLES

THESE TABLES WILL ENABLE YOU TO DISCOVER WHICH SIGNS
VENUS AND MARS OCCUPIED AT THE MOMENT OF YOUR BIRTH.
TURN TO PAGES 24–45 TO INVESTIGATE THE QUALITIES OF THESE
SIGNS, AND TO FIND OUT HOW THEY WORK WITH YOUR SUN SIGN.

The tables on pages 53–61 will enable you to discover the positions of Venus and Mars at the moment of your birth.

First find your year of birth on the top line of the appropriate table, then find your month of birth in the left-hand column. Where the column for your year of birth intersects with the row for your month of birth, you will find a group of figures and zodiacal glyphs. These figures and glyphs show which sign of the zodiac the planet occupied on the first day of that month, and any date during that month on which the planet moved into another sign.

For example, to ascertain the position of Venus on May 10, 1968, run your finger down the column marked 1968 until you reach the row for May. The row of numbers and glyphs shows that Venus occupied Aries on May 1, entered Taurus on May 4, and then moved into Gemini on May 28. Therefore, on May 10, Venus was in Taurus.

If you were born on a day when one of the planets was moving into a new sign, it may be impossible to determine your Venus and Mars signs completely accurately. If the characteristics described on the relevant pages do not seem to apply to you, read the interpretation of the sign before and after. One of these signs will be appropriate.

ZODIACAL GLYPHS

♈	Aries	♎	Libra
♉	Taurus	♏	Scorpio
♊	Gemini	♐	Sagittarius
♋	Cancer	♑	Capricorn
♌	Leo	♒	Aquarius
♍	Virgo	♓	Pisces

♀	1921	1922	1923	1924	1925	1926	1927	1928
JAN	1 ♒ 7 ♓	1 ♑ 25 ♒	1 ♏ 3 ♐	1 ♒ 20 ♓	1 ♐ 15 ♑	1 ♒	1 ♑ 10 ♒	1 ♏ 5 ♐ 30 ♏
FEB	1 ♓ 3 ♈	1 ♒ 18 ♓	1 ♐ 7 ♑ 14 ♒	1 ♑ 14 ♒	1 ♑ 8 ♒	1 ♒	1 ♒ 3 ♓ 27 ♈	1 ♑ 23 ♒
MAR	1 ♈ 8 ♉	1 ♓ 14 ♈	1 ♑ 7 ♒	1 ♒ 10 ♓	1 ♒ 5 ♓ 29 ♈	1 ♒	1 ♈ 8 ♉	1 ♒ 19 ♓
APR	1 ♉ 26 ♈	1 ♈ 7 ♉	1 ♓ 2 ♈ 27 ♉	1 ♉ 6 ♊	1 ♒ 22 ♓	1 ♒ 7 ♓	1 ♉ 17 ♊	1 ♈ 12 ♓
MAY	1 ♈	1 ♉ 2 ♊ 26 ♋	1 ♈ 22 ♉	1 ♊ 7 ♋	1 ♉ 16 ♊	1 ♓ 7 ♈	1 ♊ 13 ♋	1 ♈ 7 ♉ 31 ♊
JUN	1 ♈ 3 ♉	1 ♉ 20 ♊	1 ♋ 16 ♊	1 ♋	1 ♊ 10 ♋	1 ♈ 3 ♉ 29 ♊	1 ♊ 9 ♌	1 ♊ 24 ♋
JUL	1 ♉ 9 ♊	1 ♌ 16 ♍	1 ♊ 11 ♋	1 ♋	1 ♋ 4 ♌ 29 ♍	1 ♊ 25 ♋	1 ♌ 8 ♍	1 ♋ 19 ♌
AUG	1 ♊ 6 ♋	1 ♍ 11 ♎	1 ♋ 4 ♌ 28 ♍	1 ♋	1 ♍ 23 ♎	1 ♋ 19 ♌	1 ♍	1 ♌ 12 ♍
SEP	1 ♌ 27 ♍	1 ♎ 8 ♏	1 ♍ 22 ♎	1 ♋ 8 ♌	1 ♎ 17 ♏	1 ♌ 12 ♍	1 ♍	1 ♍ 5 ♎ 30 ♏
OCT	1 ♍ 21 ♎	1 ♏ 11 ♐	1 ♎ 16 ♏	1 ♌ 9 ♍	1 ♏ 12 ♐	1 ♍ 6 ♎ 30 ♏	1 ♍	1 ♏ 24 ♐
NOV	1 ♎ 14 ♏	1 ♐ 29 ♏	1 ♏ 9 ♐	1 ♌ 3 ♍ 28 ♎	1 ♏ 7 ♐	1 ♏ 23 ♐	1 ♍ 10 ♎	1 ♐ 18 ♑
DEC	1 ♏ 8 ♐	1 ♏	1 ♐ 3 ♑ 27 ♒	1 ♏ 22 ♐	1 ♐ 6 ♑	1 ♐ 17 ♑	1 ♎ 9 ♏	1 ♑ 13 ♒

♀	1929	1930	1931	1932	1933	1934	1935	1936
JAN	1 ♒ 7 ♓	1 ♑ 25 ♒	1 ♏ 4 ♐	1 ♒ 20 ♓	1 ♐ 15 ♑	1 ♒	1 ♑ 9 ♒	1 ♏ 4 ♐ 29 ♏
FEB	1 ♓ 3 ♈	1 ♒ 17 ♓	1 ♐ 7 ♑	1 ♓ 13 ♈	1 ♑ 8 ♒	1 ♒	1 ♒ 2 ♓ 27 ♈	1 ♑ 23 ♒
MAR	1 ♈ 9 ♉	1 ♓ 13 ♈	1 ♑ 6 ♒	1 ♓ 10 ♈	1 ♒ 4 ♓ 28 ♈	1 ♒	1 ♈ 23 ♉	1 ♒ 18 ♓
APR	1 ♉ 21 ♈	1 ♈ 7 ♉	1 ♓ 27 ♈	1 ♓ 6 ♈	1 ♈ 21 ♉	1 ♒ 7 ♓	1 ♉ 17 ♊	1 ♈ 12 ♓
MAY	1 ♈	1 ♊ 26 ♋	1 ♈ 22 ♉	1 ♊ 7 ♋	1 ♉ 16 ♊	1 ♓ 7 ♈	1 ♊ 12 ♋	1 ♈ 6 ♉ 30 ♊
JUN	1 ♈ 4 ♉	1 ♉ 20 ♊	1 ♉ 15 ♊	1 ♋	1 ♊ 9 ♋	1 ♈ 3 ♉ 29 ♊	1 ♊ 8 ♌	1 ♊ 24 ♋
JUL	1 ♉ 9 ♊	1 ♌ 15 ♍	1 ♊ 10 ♋	1 ♋	1 ♋ 4 ♌ 28 ♍	1 ♊ 24 ♋	1 ♌ 8 ♍	1 ♋ 18 ♌
AUG	1 ♊ 6 ♋	1 ♍ 11 ♎	1 ♋ 4 ♌ 28 ♍	1 ♋	1 ♍ 22 ♎	1 ♋ 18 ♌	1 ♍	1 ♌ 12 ♍
SEP	1 ♌ 26 ♍	1 ♎ 8 ♏	1 ♍ 21 ♎	1 ♋ 9 ♌	1 ♎ 16 ♏	1 ♌ 12 ♍	1 ♍	1 ♍ 5 ♎ 29 ♏
OCT	1 ♍ 21 ♎	1 ♏ 13 ♐	1 ♎ 15 ♏	1 ♌ 9 ♍	1 ♏ 12 ♐	1 ♍ 6 ♎ 30 ♏	1 ♍	1 ♏ 24 ♐
NOV	1 ♎ 14 ♏	1 ♐ 23 ♏	1 ♏ 8 ♐	1 ♌ 3 ♍ 28 ♎	1 ♏ 7 ♐	1 ♏ 23 ♐	1 ♍ 10 ♎	1 ♐ 17 ♑
DEC	1 ♏ 8 ♐ 31 ♑	1 ♏	1 ♐ 2 ♑ 26 ♒	1 ♐ 22 ♒	1 ♐ 6 ♑	1 ♐ 17 ♑	1 ♎ 9 ♏	1 ♑ 12 ♒

– VENUS TABLES –

♀	1937	1938	1939	1940	1941	1942	1943	1944
JAN	1♒ 7♓	1♐ 24♑	1♐ 5♑	1♒ 19♓	1♐ 14♑	1♒	1♑ 9♒	1♏ 4♐ 29♑
FEB	1♓ 3♈	1♑ 17♒	1♑ 7♒	1♓ 13♈	1♑ 7♒	1♒	1♒ 2♓ 26♈	1♑ 22♒
MAR	1♈ 10♉	1♒ 13♓	1♒ 6♓	1♈ 9♉	1♒ 3♓ 28♈	1♒	1♈ 22♉	1♒ 18♓
APR	1♉ 15♈	1♓ 6♈ 30♉	1♓ 26♈	1♉ 5♈	1♈ 21♉	1♒ 7♓	1♉ 16♊	1♓ 11♈
MAY	1♈	1♉ 25♊	1♈ 21♉	1♈ 7♉	1♉ 15♊	1♓ 7♈	1♊ 12♋	1♈ 5♉ 30♊
JUN	1♈ 5♉	1♊ 19♋	1♉ 15♊	1♉	1♊ 8♋	1♈ 3♉ 28♊	1♋ 8♌	1♊ 23♋
JUL	1♉ 8♊	1♋ 15♌	1♊ 10♋	1♉ 6♊	1♋ 3♌ 28♍	1♊ 24♋	1♌ 8♍	1♋ 18♌
AUG	1♊ 5♋	1♌ 10♍	1♋ 3♌ 27♍	1♊ 2♋	1♍ 22♎	1♋ 18♌	1♍	1♌ 11♍
SEP	1♋ 26♌	1♍ 8♎	1♍ 21♎	1♋ 9♌	1♎ 16♏	1♌ 11♍	1♍	1♍ 4♎ 29♏
OCT	1♌ 20♍	1♎ 14♏	1♎ 15♏	1♌ 7♍	1♏ 11♐	1♍ 5♎ 29♏	1♍	1♏ 23♐
NOV	1♍ 13♎	1♏ 16♐	1♏ 8♐	1♍ 2♎ 27♏	1♐ 7♑	1♏ 22♐	1♍ 10♎	1♐ 17♑
DEC	1♎ 7♏ 31♐	1♐	1♐ 2♑ 26♒	1♏ 21♐	1♑ 6♒	1♐ 16♑	1♎ 9♏	1♑ 12♒

♀	1945	1946	1947	1948	1949	1950	1951	1952
JAN	1♒ 6♓	1♐ 23♑	1♐ 6♑	1♒ 19♓	1♐ 14♑	1♒	1♑ 8♒	1♏ 3♐ 28♑
FEB	1♓ 3♈	1♑ 16♒	1♑ 7♒	1♓ 12♈	1♑ 7♒	1♒	1♒ 25♓	1♑ 21♒
MAR	1♈ 12♉	1♒ 12♓	1♒ 6♓ 31♈	1♈ 7♉	1♒ 3♓ 27♈	1♒	1♓ 22♈	1♒ 17♓
APR	1♉ 8♈	1♓ 6♈ 30♉	1♈ 26♉	1♉ 5♈	1♈ 20♉	1♒ 7♓	1♈ 16♉	1♓ 10♈
MAY	1♈	1♉ 25♊	1♉ 21♊	1♈ 8♉	1♉ 15♊	1♓ 6♈	1♉ 12♊	1♈ 5♉ 29♊
JUN	1♈ 5♉	1♊ 19♋	1♊ 14♋	1♉ 30♊	1♊ 8♋	1♈ 2♉ 28♊	1♊ 8♋	1♊ 23♋
JUL	1♉ 8♊	1♋ 14♌	1♋ 9♌	1♊	1♋ 2♌ 27♍	1♊ 23♋	1♋ 9♌	1♋ 17♌
AUG	1♊ 5♋	1♌ 3♍ 27♎	1♌ 3♍ 27♎	1♊ 4♋	1♍ 21♎	1♋ 17♌	1♌	1♌ 10♍
SEP	1♋ 25♌	1♎ 8♏	1♎ 20♏	1♋ 9♌	1♎ 15♏	1♌ 11♍	1♍	1♍ 4♎ 28♏
OCT	1♌ 20♍	1♏ 17♐	1♏ 14♐	1♌ 7♍	1♏ 11♐	1♍ 5♎ 29♏	1♍	1♏ 23♐
NOV	1♍ 13♎	1♐ 9♏	1♐ 7♑	1♍ 2♎ 27♏	1♐ 7♑	1♏ 22♐	1♍ 10♎	1♐ 16♑
DEC	1♎ 7♏ 31♐	1♏ 25♐	1♑ 21♒	1♏ 21♐	1♑ 7♒	1♐ 15♑	1♎ 11♏	1♑ 11♒

♀	1953	1954	1955	1956	1957	1958	1959	1960
JAN	1 ♒ 6 ♓	1 ♑ 23 ♒	1 ♏ 7 ♐	1 ♒ 18 ♓	1 ♐ 13 ♑	1 ♒	1 ♑ 8 ♒	1 ♏ 3 ♐ 28 ♑
FEB	1 ♓ 3 ♈	1 ♒ 16 ♓	1 ♐ 7 ♑	1 ♓ 12 ♈	1 ♑ 6 ♒	1 ♒	1 ♓ 25 ♈	1 ♑ 21 ♒
MAR	1 ♈ 15 ♉	1 ♓ 12 ♈	1 ♑ 5 ♒ 31 ♓	1 ♈ 8 ♉	1 ♒ 2 ♓ 26 ♈	1 ♒	1 ♈ 21 ♉	1 ♒ 16 ♓
APR	1 ♈	1 ♈ 5 ♉ 29 ♊	1 ♓ 25 ♈	1 ♉ 5 ♊	1 ♈ 19 ♉	1 ♒ 7 ♓	1 ♉ 15 ♊	1 ♓ 10 ♈
MAY	1 ♈	1 ♊ 24 ♋	1 ♈ 20 ♉	1 ♊ 9 ♋	1 ♉ 14 ♊	1 ♓ 6 ♈	1 ♊ 11 ♋	1 ♈ 4 ♉ 29 ♊
JUN	1 ♈ 6 ♉	1 ♋ 18 ♌	1 ♉ 14 ♊	1 ♋ 24 ♊	1 ♊ 7 ♋	1 ♈ 2 ♉ 27 ♊	1 ♊ 7 ♋	1 ♊ 22 ♋
JUL	1 ♉ 8 ♊	1 ♌ 14 ♍	1 ♊ 9 ♋	1 ♊	1 ♋ 2 ♌ 27 ♍	1 ♊ 22 ♋	1 ♌ 9 ♍	1 ♋ 16 ♌
AUG	1 ♊ 5 ♋ 31 ♌	1 ♍ 10 ♎	1 ♋ 2 ♌ 26 ♍	1 ♊ 5 ♋	1 ♍ 21 ♎	1 ♋ 16 ♌	1 ♍	1 ♌ 9 ♍
SEP	1 ♌ 25 ♍	1 ♎ 7 ♏	1 ♍ 19 ♎	1 ♋ 9 ♌	1 ♎ 15 ♏	1 ♌ 10 ♍	1 ♍ 21 ♎ 26 ♍	1 ♍ 3 ♎ 28 ♏
OCT	1 ♍ 19 ♎	1 ♏ 24 ♐ 28 ♏	1 ♎ 13 ♏	1 ♌ 7 ♍	1 ♏ 11 ♐	1 ♍ 3 ♎ 28 ♏	1 ♍	1 ♏ 22 ♐
NOV	1 ♎ 12 ♏	1 ♏	1 ♏	1 ♏ 6 ♐	1 ♐ 26 ♑	1 ♏ 21 ♐	1 ♍ 10 ♎	1 ♐ 16 ♑
DEC	1 ♏ 6 ♐ 30 ♑	1 ♏	1 ♑ 25 ♒	1 ♏ 20 ♐	1 ♑ 7 ♒	1 ♐ 15 ♑	1 ♎ 8 ♏	1 ♑ 11 ♒

♀	1961	1962	1963	1964	1965	1966	1967	1968
JAN	1 ♒ 6 ♓	1 ♑ 22 ♒	1 ♏ 7 ♐	1 ♒ 17 ♓	1 ♐ 13 ♑	1 ♒	1 ♑ 7 ♒ 31 ♓	1 ♏ 2 ♐ 27 ♑
FEB	1 ♓ 3 ♈	1 ♒ 15 ♓	1 ♐ 6 ♑	1 ♓ 11 ♈	1 ♑ 6 ♒	1 ♒ 7 ♑ 26 ♒	1 ♓ 24 ♈	1 ♑ 21 ♒
MAR	1 ♈	1 ♓ 11 ♈	1 ♑ 5 ♒ 31 ♓	1 ♈ 8 ♉	1 ♒ 2 ♓ 26 ♈	1 ♒	1 ♈ 21 ♉	1 ♒ 16 ♓
APR	1 ♈	1 ♈ 5 ♉ 29 ♊	1 ♓ 25 ♈	1 ♉ 5 ♊	1 ♈ 19 ♉	1 ♒ 7 ♓	1 ♉ 15 ♊	1 ♓ 9 ♈
MAY	1 ♈	1 ♊ 24 ♋	1 ♈ 19 ♉	1 ♊ 10 ♋	1 ♉ 13 ♊	1 ♓ 6 ♈	1 ♊ 11 ♋	1 ♈ 4 ♉ 28 ♊
JUN	1 ♈ 6 ♉	1 ♋ 18 ♌	1 ♉ 13 ♊	1 ♋ 18 ♊	1 ♊ 7 ♋	1 ♉ 27 ♊	1 ♊ 7 ♋	1 ♊ 21 ♋
JUL	1 ♉ 8 ♊	1 ♌ 13 ♍	1 ♊ 8 ♋	1 ♊	1 ♋ 26 ♌	1 ♊ 22 ♋	1 ♌ 9 ♍	1 ♋ 16 ♌
AUG	1 ♊ 4 ♋ 30 ♌	1 ♍ 26 ♎	1 ♌ 6 ♍	1 ♊ 6 ♋	1 ♌ 20 ♍	1 ♋ 16 ♌	1 ♍	1 ♌ 9 ♍
SEP	1 ♌ 24 ♍	1 ♍ 8 ♎	1 ♍ 18 ♎	1 ♋ 9 ♌	1 ♍ 14 ♎	1 ♌ 9 ♍	1 ♍ 10 ♌	1 ♍ 3 ♎ 27 ♏
OCT	1 ♍ 18 ♎	1 ♏	1 ♎ 13 ♏	1 ♌ 6 ♍	1 ♍ 10 ♎	1 ♍ 3 ♎ 27 ♏	1 ♌ 2 ♍	1 ♏ 22 ♐
NOV	1 ♎ 12 ♏	1 ♏	1 ♏ 6 ♐ 30 ♑	1 ♎ 25 ♏	1 ♏ 6 ♐	1 ♏ 20 ♐	1 ♍ 10 ♎	1 ♐ 15 ♑
DEC	1 ♏ 6 ♐ 29 ♑	1 ♏	1 ♑ 24 ♒	1 ♏ 20 ♐	1 ♑ 8 ♒	1 ♐ 14 ♑	1 ♎ 8 ♏	1 ♑ 10 ♒

♀	1969	1970	1971	1972	1973	1974	1975	1976
JAN	1 5 ♒ ♓	1 22 ♑ ♒	1 8 ♏ ♐	1 17 ♒ ♓	1 12 ♐ ♑	1 30 ♒ ♑	1 7 31 ♑ ♒ ♓	1 2 27 ♏ ♐ ♑
FEB	1 3 ♓ ♈	1 15 ♒ ♓	1 6 ♐ ♑	1 11 ♓ ♈	1 5 ♑ ♒	1 ♑	1 24 ♓ ♈	1 20 ♑ ♒
MAR	1 ♈	1 11 ♓ ♈	1 5 30 ♑ ♒ ♓	1 8 ♈ ♉	1 25 ♓ ♈	1 ♒	1 20 ♈ ♉	1 15 ♒ ♓
APR	1 ♈	1 4 28 ♈ ♉ ♊	1 23 ♓ ♈	1 4 ♉ ♊	1 19 ♈ ♉	1 7 ♒ ♓	1 14 ♉ ♊	1 9 ♓ ♈
MAY	1 ♈	1 23 ♊ ♋	1 19 ♈ ♉	1 11 ♊ ♋	1 13 ♉ ♊	1 5 ♓ ♈	1 10 ♊ ♋	1 3 27 ♈ ♉ ♊
JUN	1 6 ♈ ♉	1 17 ♋ ♌	1 13 ♉ ♊	1 12 ♋ ♊	1 6 ♊ ♋	1 26 ♉ ♊	1 7 ♋ ♌	1 21 ♊ ♋
JUL	1 8 ♉ ♊	1 13 ♌ ♍	1 7 ♊ ♋	1 ♊	1 26 ♌ ♍	1 22 ♊ ♋	1 10 ♌ ♍	1 15 ♋ ♌
AUG	1 4 30 ♊ ♋ ♌	1 9 ♍ ♎	1 25 ♌ ♍	1 7 ♊ ♋	1 19 ♍ ♎	1 15 ♋ ♌	1 ♍	1 9 ♌ ♍
SEP	1 24 ♌ ♍	1 8 ♎ ♏	1 18 ♍ ♎	1 8 ♋ ♌	1 14 ♎ ♏	1 9 ♌ ♍	1 3 ♍ ♌	1 2 26 ♍ ♎ ♏
OCT	1 18 ♍ ♎	1 ♏	1 12 ♎ ♏	1 6 31 ♌ ♍ ♎	1 10 ♏ ♐	1 3 27 ♍ ♎ ♏	1 5 ♌ ♍	1 21 ♏ ♐
NOV	1 11 ♎ ♏	1 ♏	1 5 30 ♏ ♐ ♑	1 25 ♎ ♏	1 6 ♐ ♑	1 20 ♏ ♐	1 10 ♍ ♎	1 15 ♐ ♑
DEC	1 5 29 ♏ ♐ ♑	1 ♏	1 24 ♑ ♒	1 19 ♏ ♐	1 8 ♑ ♒	1 14 ♐ ♑	1 7 ♎ ♏	1 10 ♑ ♒

♀	1977	1978	1979	1980	1981	1982	1983	1984
JAN	1 5 ♒ ♓	1 21 ♑ ♒	1 8 ♏ ♐	1 16 ♒ ♓	1 12 ♐ ♑	1 24 ♒ ♑	1 6 30 ♑ ♒ ♓	1 2 26 ♏ ♐ ♑
FEB	1 3 ♓ ♈	1 14 ♒ ♓	1 6 ♐ ♑	1 10 ♓ ♈	1 5 28 ♑ ♒ ♓	1 ♑	1 23 ♓ ♈	1 20 ♑ ♒
MAR	1 ♈	1 10 ♓ ♈	1 4 29 ♑ ♒ ♓	1 7 ♈ ♉	1 25 ♓ ♈	1 3 ♑ ♒	1 20 ♈ ♉	1 15 ♒ ♓
APR	1 ♈	1 3 28 ♈ ♉ ♊	1 23 ♓ ♈	1 4 ♉ ♊	1 18 ♈ ♉	1 7 ♒ ♓	1 14 ♉ ♊	1 8 ♓ ♈
MAY	1 ♈	1 22 ♊ ♋	1 18 ♈ ♉	1 13 ♊ ♋	1 12 ♉ ♊	1 5 31 ♓ ♈ ♉	1 10 ♊ ♋	1 3 27 ♈ ♉ ♊
JUN	1 6 ♈ ♉	1 17 ♋ ♌	1 12 ♉ ♊	1 6 ♋ ♊	1 6 30 ♊ ♋ ♌	1 26 ♉ ♊	1 7 ♋ ♌	1 21 ♊ ♋
JUL	1 8 ♉ ♊	1 12 ♌ ♍	1 7 31 ♊ ♋ ♌	1 ♊	1 25 ♌ ♍	1 21 ♊ ♋	1 11 ♌ ♍	1 15 ♋ ♌
AUG	1 3 29 ♊ ♋ ♌	1 8 ♍ ♎	1 25 ♌ ♍	1 7 ♊ ♋	1 19 ♍ ♎	1 15 ♋ ♌	1 28 ♍ ♌	1 8 ♌ ♍
SEP	1 23 ♌ ♍	1 8 ♎ ♏	1 18 ♍ ♎	1 8 ♋ ♌	1 13 ♎ ♏	1 8 ♌ ♍	1 ♌	1 2 26 ♍ ♎ ♏
OCT	1 17 ♍ ♎	1 ♏	1 12 ♎ ♏	1 5 31 ♌ ♍ ♎	1 9 ♏ ♐	1 2 26 ♍ ♎ ♏	1 6 ♌ ♍	1 21 ♏ ♐
NOV	1 11 ♎ ♏	1 ♏	1 5 29 ♏ ♐ ♑	1 25 ♎ ♏	1 6 ♐ ♑	1 19 ♏ ♐	1 10 ♍ ♎	1 14 ♐ ♑
DEC	1 4 28 ♏ ♐ ♑	1 ♏	1 23 ♑ ♒	1 19 ♏ ♐	1 9 ♑ ♒	1 12 ♐ ♑	1 7 ♎ ♏	1 10 ♑ ♒

♀ 1985–1992

♀	1985	1986	1987	1988	1989	1990	1991	1992
JAN	1 ♒ 5 ♓	1 ♑ 21 ♒	1 ♏ 8 ♐	1 ♒ 16 ♓	1 ♐ 11 ♑	1 ♒ 17 ♑	1 ♑ 6 ♒ 30 ♓	1 ♐ 26 ♑
FEB	1 ♓ 3 ♈	1 ♒ 14 ♓	1 ♐ 6 ♑	1 ♑ 10 ♒	1 ♑ 4 ♒ 28 ♓	1 ♑	1 ♓ 23 ♈	1 ♑ 19 ♒
MAR	1 ♈	1 ♓ 9 ♈	1 ♑ 4 ♒ 29 ♓	1 ♈ 7 ♉	1 ♓ 24 ♈	1 ♑ 4 ♒	1 ♈ 19 ♉	1 ♒ 14 ♓
APR	1 ♈	1 ♈ 8 ♉ 27 ♊	1 ♒ 23 ♈	1 ♉ 4 ♊	1 ♈ 17 ♉	1 ♒ 7 ♓	1 ♉ 13 ♊	1 ♓ 7 ♈
MAY	1 ♈	1 ♊ 22 ♋	1 ♈ 18 ♉	1 ♈ 18 ♉ 27 ♊	1 ♉ 12 ♊	1 ♓ 4 ♈ 31 ♉	1 ♉ 9 ♋	1 ♈ 2 ♉ 26 ♊
JUN	1 ♈ 7 ♉	1 ♋ 16 ♌	1 ♉ 12 ♊	1 ♊	1 ♊ 5 ♋ 30 ♌	1 ♉ 25 ♊	1 ♋ 7 ♌	1 ♊ 20 ♋
JUL	1 ♉ 7 ♊	1 ♌ 12 ♍	1 ♊ 6 ♋ 31 ♌	1 ♊	1 ♌ 24 ♍	1 ♊ 20 ♋	1 ♌ 11 ♍	1 ♋ 14 ♌
AUG	1 ♊ 3 ♋ 28 ♌	1 ♍ 8 ♎	1 ♌ 24 ♍	1 ♊ 7 ♋	1 ♍ 18 ♎	1 ♋ 13 ♌	1 ♍ 22 ♌	1 ♌ 2 ♍
SEP	1 ♌ 23 ♍	1 ♎ 8 ♏	1 ♍ 17 ♎	1 ♋ 8 ♌	1 ♌ 13 ♎	1 ♌ 9 ♍	1 ♌	1 ♌ 25 ♍
OCT	1 ♍ 17 ♎	1 ♏	1 ♎ 11 ♏	1 ♌ 5 ♍ 30 ♎	1 ♏ 9 ♐	1 ♍ 2 ♎ 26 ♏	1 ♌ 7 ♍	1 ♏ 20 ♐
NOV	1 ♎ 10 ♏	1 ♏	1 ♏ 4 ♐ 28 ♑	1 ♎ 24 ♏	1 ♐ 6 ♑	1 ♏ 19 ♐	1 ♍ 9 ♎	1 ♐ 14 ♑
DEC	1 ♏ 4 ♐ 28 ♑	1 ♏	1 ♑ 23 ♒	1 ♏ 18 ♐	1 ♑ 10 ♒	1 ♐ 13 ♑	1 ♎ 7 ♏	1 ♑ 9 ♒

♀ 1993–2000

♀	1993	1994	1995	1996	1997	1998	1999	2000
JAN	1 ♒ 4 ♓	1 ♑ 20 ♒	1 ♏ 8 ♐	1 ♒ 15 ♓	1 ♐ 10 ♑	1 ♒ 10 ♑	1 ♑ 5 ♒ 29 ♓	1 ♐ 25 ♑
FEB	1 ♓ 3 ♈	1 ♒ 13 ♓	1 ♐ 5 ♑	1 ♑ 9 ♒	1 ♑ 4 ♒ 28 ♓	1 ♑	1 ♓ 22 ♈	1 ♑ 19 ♒
MAR	1 ♈	1 ♓ 9 ♈	1 ♑ 3 ♒ 29 ♓	1 ♈ 6 ♉	1 ♓ 24 ♈	1 ♑ 5 ♒	1 ♈ 19 ♉	1 ♒ 14 ♓
APR	1 ♈	1 ♈ 2 ♉ 27 ♊	1 ♓ 23 ♈	1 ♉ 4 ♊	1 ♈ 17 ♉	1 ♒ 7 ♓	1 ♉ 13 ♊	1 ♓ 7 ♈
MAY	1 ♈	1 ♊ 21 ♋	1 ♈ 17 ♉	1 ♊	1 ♉ 11 ♊	1 ♓ 4 ♈ 30 ♉	1 ♊ 9 ♋	1 ♈ 2 ♉ 26 ♊
JUN	1 ♈ 7 ♉	1 ♋ 15 ♌	1 ♉ 11 ♊	1 ♊	1 ♊ 4 ♋ 29 ♌	1 ♉ 25 ♊	1 ♋ 6 ♌	1 ♊ 19 ♋
JUL	1 ♉ 6 ♊	1 ♌ 12 ♍	1 ♊ 6 ♋ 30 ♌	1 ♊	1 ♌ 24 ♍	1 ♊ 20 ♋	1 ♌ 13 ♍	1 ♋ 14 ♌
AUG	1 ♊ 2 ♋ 28 ♌	1 ♍ 8 ♎	1 ♌ 23 ♍	1 ♊ 8 ♋	1 ♍ 18 ♎	1 ♋ 14 ♌	1 ♍ 16 ♌	1 ♌ 7 ♍
SEP	1 ♌ 22 ♍	1 ♎ 8 ♏	1 ♍ 17 ♎	1 ♋ 8 ♌	1 ♌ 12 ♎	1 ♌ 7 ♍	1 ♌	1 ♌ 25 ♍
OCT	1 ♍ 16 ♎	1 ♏	1 ♎ 11 ♏	1 ♌ 5 ♍ 30 ♎	1 ♏ 9 ♐	1 ♎ 25 ♏	1 ♌ 8 ♍	1 ♏ 20 ♐
NOV	1 ♎ 9 ♏	1 ♏	1 ♏ 4 ♐ 28 ♑	1 ♎ 23 ♏	1 ♐ 6 ♑	1 ♏ 18 ♐	1 ♍ 10 ♎	1 ♐ 13 ♑
DEC	1 ♏ 3 ♐ 27 ♑	1 ♏	1 ♑ 22 ♒	1 ♏ 17 ♐	1 ♑ 12 ♒	1 ♐ 12 ♑	1 ♎ 6 ♏	1 ♑ 9 ♒

Mars Tables (1921–1930). Zodiac sign entries with ingress dates (♈ Aries, ♉ Taurus, ♊ Gemini, ♋ Cancer, ♌ Leo, ♍ Virgo, ♎ Libra, ♏ Scorpio, ♐ Sagittarius, ♑ Capricorn, ♒ Aquarius, ♓ Pisces).

♂	1921	1922	1923	1924	1925	1926	1927	1928	1929	1930
JAN	1 ♒ 5 ♓	1 ♏	1 ♓ 21 ♈	1 ♏ 19 ♐	1 ♈	1 ♐	1 ♉	1 ♐ 19 ♑	1 ♊	1 ♑
FEB	1 ♓ 13 ♈	1 ♏ 18 ♐	1 ♈	1 ♐	1 ♈ 5 ♉	1 ♐ 9 ♑	1 ♉ 22 ♊	1 ♑ 28 ♒	1 ♊	1 ♑ 6 ♒
MAR	1 ♈ 25 ♉	1 ♐	1 ♈ 4 ♉	1 ♐ 6 ♑	1 ♉ 24 ♊	1 ♑ 23 ♒	1 ♊	1 ♒	1 ♊ 10 ♋	1 ♒ 17 ♓
APR	1 ♉	1 ♐	1 ♉ 16 ♊	1 ♑ 24 ♒	1 ♊	1 ♒	1 ♊ 17 ♋	1 ♒ 7 ♓	1 ♋	1 ♓ 24 ♈
MAY	1 ♉ 6 ♊	1 ♐	1 ♊ 30 ♋	1 ♒	1 ♊ 9 ♋	1 ♒ 3 ♓	1 ♋	1 ♓ 16 ♈	1 ♋ 13 ♌	1 ♈
JUN	1 ♊ 18 ♋	1 ♐	1 ♋	1 ♒ 24 ♓	1 ♋	1 ♓ 26 ♈	1 ♋	1 ♈ 26 ♉	1 ♌ 26 ♍	1 ♈ 3 ♉
JUL	1 ♋	1 ♐	1 ♋ 16 ♌	1 ♓	1 ♌	1 ♈	1 ♋ 25 ♌	1 ♉	1 ♍	1 ♉ 14 ♊
AUG	1 ♋ 3 ♌	1 ♐	1 ♌ 24 ♍	1 ♓ 12 ♒	1 ♌ 12 ♍	1 ♈	1 ♌	1 ♉ 9 ♊	1 ♍ 21 ♎	1 ♊ 28 ♋
SEP	1 ♌ 19 ♍	1 ♐ 13 ♑	1 ♍	1 ♒	1 ♍	1 ♈ 28 ♉	1 ♌ 10 ♍	1 ♊	1 ♎	1 ♋
OCT	1 ♍	1 ♑ 30 ♒	1 ♍ 18 ♎	1 ♒	1 ♍ 28 ♎	1 ♉	1 ♍ 26 ♎	1 ♊ 3 ♋	1 ♎ 6 ♏	1 ♋ 20 ♌
NOV	1 ♍ 6 ♎	1 ♒	1 ♎	1 ♒	1 ♎	1 ♉	1 ♎	1 ♋	1 ♏ 18 ♐	1 ♌
DEC	1 ♎ 26 ♏	1 ♒ 11 ♓	1 ♎ 4 ♏	1 ♒ 19 ♓	1 ♎ 28 ♏	1 ♉	1 ♎ 8 ♏	1 ♋ 20 ♊	1 ♐ 29 ♑	1 ♌

Mars Tables (1931–1940).

♂	1931	1932	1933	1934	1935	1936	1937	1938	1939	1940
JAN	1 ♌	1 ♑ 18 ♒	1 ♍	1 ♒	1 ♎	1 ♒ 14 ♓	1 ♎ 5 ♏	1 ♓ 30 ♈	1 ♏ 29 ♐	1 ♓ 4 ♈
FEB	1 ♌ 16 ♋	1 ♒ 25 ♓	1 ♍	1 ♒ 4 ♓	1 ♎	1 ♓ 22 ♈	1 ♏	1 ♈	1 ♐	1 ♈ 17 ♉
MAR	1 ♋ 30 ♌	1 ♓	1 ♍	1 ♓ 14 ♈	1 ♎	1 ♈	1 ♏ 13 ♐	1 ♈ 12 ♉	1 ♐ 21 ♑	1 ♉
APR	1 ♌	1 ♓ 3 ♈	1 ♍	1 ♈ 22 ♉	1 ♎	1 ♉	1 ♐	1 ♉ 23 ♊	1 ♑	1 ♊
MAY	1 ♌	1 ♈ 12 ♉	1 ♍	1 ♉	1 ♎	1 ♉ 13 ♊	1 ♐ 14 ♏	1 ♊	1 ♑ 25 ♒	1 ♊ 17 ♋
JUN	1 ♌ 10 ♍	1 ♉ 8 ♊	1 ♍	1 ♉ 2 ♊	1 ♎	1 ♊ 25 ♋	1 ♏	1 ♊ 7 ♋	1 ♒	1 ♋
JUL	1 ♍	1 ♊	1 ♍ 6 ♎	1 ♊ 15 ♋	1 ♎ 29 ♏	1 ♋	1 ♏	1 ♋ 22 ♌	1 ♒	1 ♋ 3 ♌
AUG	1 ♎	1 ♊ 4 ♋	1 ♎ 26 ♏	1 ♋ 30 ♌	1 ♏	1 ♋ 10 ♌	1 ♏ 8 ♐	1 ♌	1 ♒	1 ♌ 19 ♍
SEP	1 ♎ 17 ♏	1 ♋ 20 ♌	1 ♏	1 ♌	1 ♏ 16 ♐	1 ♌ 26 ♍	1 ♐ 30 ♑	1 ♌ 7 ♍	1 ♒	1 ♍
OCT	1 ♏ 30 ♐	1 ♌	1 ♏ 9 ♐	1 ♌ 18 ♍	1 ♐ 28 ♑	1 ♍	1 ♑	1 ♍ 25 ♎	1 ♒	1 ♍ 5 ♎
NOV	1 ♐	1 ♌ 13 ♍	1 ♐ 19 ♑	1 ♍	1 ♑	1 ♍ 14 ♎	1 ♑ 11 ♒	1 ♎	1 ♒	1 ♎ 20 ♏
DEC	1 ♐ 10 ♑	1 ♍	1 ♑	1 ♍ 11 ♎	1 ♑ 7 ♒	1 ♎ 21 ♏	1 ♒ 21 ♓	1 ♎ 11 ♏	1 ♒ 19 ♓	1 ♏

♂	1941	1942	1943	1944	1945	1946	1947	1948	1949	1950
JAN	1♏ 4♐	1♈ ♉	1♐ 26♑	1♊	1♐ 5♑	1♋	1♑ 25♒	1♍	1♑ 4♒	1♎
FEB	1♐ 17♑	1♉	1♑	1♊	1♑ 14♒	1♋	1♒	1♍ 12♌	1♒ 11♓	1♎
MAR	1♑	1♉ 7♊	1♑ 8♒	1♊ 28♋	1♒ 25♓	1♋	1♒ 4♓	1♌	1♓ 21♈	1♎ 28♍
APR	1♑ 2♒	1♊ 26♋	1♒ 17♓	1♋	1♓	1♋ 22♌	1♓ 11♈	1♌	1♈ 30♉	1♍
MAY	1♒ 16♓	1♋	1♓ 27♈	1♋ 22♌	1♓ 3♈	1♌	1♈ 21♉	1♌ 18♍	1♉	1♍
JUN	1♓	1♋ 14♌	1♈	1♌	1♈ 11♉	1♌ 20♍	1♉	1♍	1♉ 10♊	1♍ 11♎
JUL	1♓ 2♈	1♌	1♈ 7♉	1♌ 12♍	1♉ 23♊	1♍	1♊	1♍ 17♎	1♊ 23♋	1♎
AUG	1♈	1♍	1♉ 23♊	1♍ 29♎	1♊	1♍ 9♎	1♊ 13♋	1♎	1♋	1♎ 10♏
SEP	1♈	1♍ 17♎	1♊	1♎	1♊ 7♋	1♎ 24♏	1♋	1♎ 3♏	1♋ 7♌	1♏ 25♐
OCT	1♈	1♎	1♊	1♎ 13♏	1♋	1♏	1♌	1♏ 17♐	1♌ 27♍	1♐
NOV	1♈	1♎ 2♏	1♊	1♏ 25♐	1♋ 11♌	1♏ 6♐	1♌	1♐ 26♑	1♍	1♐ 6♑
DEC	1♈	1♏ 15♐	1♊	1♐	1♌ 26♋	1♐ 17♑	1♍	1♑	1♍ 26♎	1♑ 15♒

♂	1951	1952	1953	1954	1955	1956	1957	1958	1959	1960
JAN	1♒ 22♓	1♎ 20♏	1♓	1♏	1♓ 15♈	1♏ 14♐	1♈ 28♉	1♐	1♉	1♐ 14♑
FEB	1♓	1♏	1♓ 8♈	1♏ 9♐	1♈ 26♉	1♐ 28♑	1♉	1♐ 3♑	1♉ 10♊	1♑ 23♒
MAR	1♓ 2♈	1♏	1♈ 20♉	1♐	1♉	1♑	1♉ 17♊	1♑ 17♒	1♊	1♒
APR	1♈ 10♉	1♏	1♉	1♐ 12♑	1♉ 10♊	1♑ 14♒	1♊	1♒ 27♓	1♊ 10♋	1♒ 2♓
MAY	1♉ 21♊	1♏	1♊	1♑	1♊ 26♋	1♒	1♊ 4♋	1♓	1♋	1♓ 11♈
JUN	1♊	1♏	1♊ 14♋	1♑	1♋	1♒ 3♓	1♋ 21♌	1♓ 7♈	1♋ 2♌	1♈ 20♉
JUL	1♊ 3♋	1♏	1♋ 29♌	1♑ 3♒	1♋ 11♌	1♓	1♌	1♈ 21♉	1♌ 20♍	1♉
AUG	1♋ 18♌	1♏ 27♐	1♌	1♒ 24♑	1♌ 27♍	1♓	1♌ 8♍	1♉	1♍	1♉ 2♊
SEP	1♌	1♐	1♌ 14♍	1♑	1♍	1♓	1♍ 24♎	1♉ 21♊	1♍ 5♎	1♊ 21♋
OCT	1♌ 5♍	1♐ 12♑	1♍	1♑ 21♒	1♍ 13♎	1♓	1♎	1♊ 29♉	1♎ 21♏	1♋
NOV	1♍ 24♎	1♑ 21♒	1♎	1♒	1♎ 29♏	1♓	1♎ 8♏	1♉	1♏	1♋
DEC	1♎	1♒ 30♓	1♎ 20♏	1♒ 4♓	1♏	1♓ 6♈	1♏ 23♐	1♉	1♏ 3♐	1♋

♂	1961	1962	1963	1964	1965	1966	1967	1968	1969	1970
JAN	1 ♋	1 ♑	1 ♌	1 / 13 ♑ ♒	1 ♍	1 / 30 ♒ ♓	1 ♎	1 / 9 ♒ ♓	1 ♏	1 / 24 ♓ ♈
FEB	1 / 5 / 7 ♋ ♊ ♋	1 / 2 ♑ ♒	1 ♌	1 / 20 ♒ ♓	1 ♍	1 ♓	1 / 12 ♎ ♏	1 / 17 ♓ ♈	1 / 25 ♏ ♐	1 ♈
MAR	1 ♋	1 / 12 ♒ ♓	1 ♌	1 / 29 ♓ ♈	1 ♍	1 ♓ ♈	1 / 31 ♏ ♎	1 ♈ ♉	1 ♐	1 / 7 ♈ ♉
APR	1 ♋	1 / 19 ♓ ♈	1 ♌	1 ♈	1 ♍	1 / 17 ♈ ♉	1 ♎	1 ♉	1 ♐	1 / 18 ♉ ♊
MAY	1 / 6 ♋ ♌	1 / 28 ♈ ♉	1 ♌	1 / 7 ♈ ♉	1 ♍	1 / 28 ♉ ♊	1 ♎	1 / 8 ♉ ♊	1 ♐	1 ♊
JUN	1 / 28 ♌ ♍	1 ♉	1 / 3 ♌ ♍	1 / 8 ♉ ♊	1 / 29 ♍ ♎	1 ♊	1 ♎	1 / 21 ♊ ♋	1 ♐	1 / 2 ♊ ♋
JUL	1 ♍	1 / 9 ♉ ♊	1 / 27 ♍ ♎	1 / 30 ♊ ♋	1 ♎	1 / 11 ♊ ♋	1 / 19 ♎ ♏	1 ♋	1 ♐	1 / 18 ♋ ♌
AUG	1 / 17 ♍ ♎	1 / 22 ♊ ♋	1 ♎	1 ♋	1 ♎	1 / 20 ♋ ♌	1 ♏	1 ♏	1 / 5 ♐	1 ♌
SEP	1 ♎	1 ♋	1 / 12 ♎ ♏	1 / 15 ♋ ♌	1 ♋	1 ♌	1 / 10 ♏ ♐	1 / 21 ♏ ♐	1 / 21 ♐ ♑	1 / 3 ♌ ♍
OCT	1 / 2 ♎ ♏	1 / 11 ♋ ♌	1 / 25 ♏ ♐	1 ♌	1 / 4 ♏ ♐	1 / 12 ♌ ♍	1 / 23 ♐ ♑	1 ♐	1 ♑	1 / 20 ♍ ♎
NOV	1 / 13 ♏ ♐	1 ♌	1 ♐	1 ♌	1 / 6 ♐ ♑	1 / 14 ♍ ♎	1 ♐	1 ♑	1 / 9 ♑ ♒	1 / 4 ♍ ♎	1 ♎
DEC	1 / 24 ♐ ♑	1 ♌	1 ♐	1 ♐ ♑	1 / 23 ♑ ♒	1 / 4 ♍ ♎	1 / 2 ♑ ♒	1 / 30 ♎ ♏	1 / 15 ♒ ♓	1 / 6 ♎ ♏

♂	1971	1972	1973	1974	1975	1976	1977	1978	1979	1980
JAN	1 / 23 ♏ ♐	1 ♈	1 ♐	1 ♉	1 / 21 ♐ ♑	1 ♊	1 ♑	1 / 26 ♌ ♍	1 / 21 ♑ ♒	1 ♍
FEB	1 ♐	1 / 10 ♈ ♉	1 / 12 ♐ ♑	1 / 27 ♉ ♊	1 ♑	1 ♊	1 / 9 ♑ ♒	1 ♌	1 / 28 ♒ ♓	1 ♍
MAR	1 / 12 ♐ ♑	1 / 27 ♉ ♊	1 / 27 ♑ ♒	1 ♊	1 / 3 ♑ ♒	1 / 18 ♊ ♋	1 / 20 ♒ ♓	1 ♌	1 ♓	1 / 12 ♍ ♌
APR	1 ♑	1 ♊	1 ♒	1 / 20 ♊ ♋	1 / 11 ♒ ♓	1 ♋	1 / 28 ♓ ♈	1 / 11 ♌ ♍	1 / 7 ♓ ♈	1 ♌
MAY	1 / 3 ♑ ♒	1 / 12 ♊ ♋	1 / 8 ♒ ♓	1 ♋	1 / 21 ♓ ♈	1 / 16 ♋ ♌	1 ♈	1 ♌	1 / 16 ♈ ♉	1 / 4 ♌ ♍
JUN	1 ♒	1 / 28 ♋ ♌	1 / 21 ♓ ♈	1 / 9 ♋ ♌	1 ♈	1 ♌	1 / 6 ♈ ♉	1 / 14 ♌ ♍	1 / 26 ♉ ♊	1 ♍
JUL	1 ♒	1 ♌	1 ♈	1 / 27 ♌ ♍	1 ♉	1 / 7 ♌ ♍	1 / 18 ♉ ♊	1 ♍	1 ♊	1 / 11 ♍ ♎
AUG	1 ♒	1 / 15 ♌ ♍	1 / 12 ♈ ♉	1 ♍	1 / 14 ♉ ♊	1 / 24 ♍ ♎	1 ♊	1 / 4 ♍ ♎	1 / 8 ♊ ♋	1 / 29 ♍ ♎
SEP	1 ♒	1 ♍	1 ♉	1 / 12 ♍ ♎	1 ♉	1 ♎	1 ♋	1 / 20 ♎ ♏	1 / 25 ♋ ♌	1 ♏
OCT	1 ♒	1 ♎	1 / 30 ♉ ♈	1 ♎ ♏	1 / 17 ♉ ♊	1 ♊ ♋	1 / 27 ♋ ♌	1 ♏	1 ♌	1 / 7 ♏ ♐
NOV	1 / 6 ♒ ♓	1 / 15 ♎ ♏	1 ♈	1 ♏	1 / 26 ♋ ♊	1 / 21 ♊ ♋	1 ♌	1 / 2 ♏ ♐	1 / 20 ♌ ♍	1 / 22 ♐ ♑
DEC	1 / 26 ♓ ♈	1 / 30 ♏ ♐	1 / 24 ♈ ♉	1 / 11 ♏ ♐	1 ♊	1 ♐	1 ♌	1 ♐ ♑	1 / 13 ♍ ♎	1 / 31 ♑ ♒

– MARS TABLES –

♂	1981	1982	1983	1984	1985	1986	1987	1988	1989	1990
JAN	1 ♒	1 ♎	1 ♒ 17 ♓	1 ♎ 11 ♏	1 ♓	1 ♏	1 ♓ 8 ♈	1 ♏ 8 ♐	1 ♈ 19 ♉	1 ♐ 30 ♑
FEB	1 ♒ 7 ♓	1 ♎	1 ♓ 25 ♈	1 ♏	1 ♓ 2 ♈	1 ♏ 2 ♐	1 ♈ 21 ♉	1 ♐ 22 ♑	1 ♉	1 ♑
MAR	1 ♓ 17 ♈	1 ♎	1 ♈	1 ♏	1 ♈ 15 ♉	1 ♐ 28 ♑	1 ♉	1 ♑	1 ♉ 11 ♊	1 ♑ 12 ♒
APR	1 ♈ 25 ♉	1 ♎	1 ♈ 5 ♉	1 ♏	1 ♉ 26 ♊	1 ♑	1 ♉ 5 ♊	1 ♑ 7 ♒	1 ♊ 29 ♋	1 ♒ 21 ♓
MAY	1 ♉	1 ♎	1 ♉ 17 ♊	1 ♏	1 ♊	1 ♑	1 ♊ 21 ♋	1 ♒ 22 ♓	1 ♋	1 ♓ 31 ♈
JUN	1 ♉ 5 ♊	1 ♎	1 ♊ 29 ♋	1 ♏	1 ♊ 9 ♋	1 ♑	1 ♋	1 ♓	1 ♋ 17 ♌	1 ♈
JUL	1 ♊ 18 ♋	1 ♎	1 ♋	1 ♏	1 ♋ 25 ♌	1 ♑	1 ♋ 7 ♌	1 ♓ 14 ♈	1 ♌	1 ♈ 13 ♉
AUG	1 ♋	1 ♎ 3 ♏	1 ♋ 14 ♌	1 ♏ 18 ♐	1 ♌	1 ♑	1 ♌ 23 ♍	1 ♈	1 ♌ 3 ♍	1 ♉ 31 ♊
SEP	1 ♋ 2 ♌	1 ♏ 20 ♐	1 ♌ 30 ♍	1 ♐	1 ♌ 10 ♍	1 ♑	1 ♍	1 ♈	1 ♍ 20 ♎	1 ♊
OCT	1 ♌ 21 ♍	1 ♐	1 ♍	1 ♐ 5 ♑	1 ♍ 28 ♎	1 ♑ 9 ♒	1 ♍ 9 ♎	1 ♈ 24 ♓	1 ♎	1 ♊
NOV	1 ♍	1 ♑	1 ♍ 18 ♎	1 ♑ 16 ♒	1 ♎	1 ♒ 26 ♓	1 ♎ 24 ♏	1 ♓ 2 ♈	1 ♎ 4 ♏	1 ♊
DEC	1 ♍ 16 ♎	1 ♑ 10 ♒	1 ♎	1 ♒ 25 ♓	1 ♎ 15 ♏	1 ♓	1 ♏	1 ♈	1 ♏ 18 ♐	1 ♊ 14 ♉

♂	1991	1992	1993	1994	1995	1996	1997	1998	1999	2000
JAN	1 ♉ 21 ♊	1 ♐ 9 ♑	1 ♋	1 ♑ 28 ♒	1 ♍ 23 ♌	1 ♑ 9 ♒	1 ♍ 3 ♎	1 ♒ 25 ♓	1 ♎ 26 ♏	1 ♒ 4 ♓
FEB	1 ♊	1 ♑ 18 ♒	1 ♋	1 ♒	1 ♌	1 ♒ 15 ♓	1 ♎	1 ♓	1 ♏	1 ♓ 12 ♈
MAR	1 ♊	1 ♒ 28 ♓	1 ♋	1 ♒ 7 ♓	1 ♌	1 ♓ 25 ♈	1 ♎ 9 ♍	1 ♓ 5 ♈	1 ♏	1 ♈ 23 ♉
APR	1 ♊ 3 ♋	1 ♓	1 ♋ 28 ♌	1 ♓ 15 ♈	1 ♌	1 ♈	1 ♍	1 ♈ 13 ♉	1 ♏	1 ♉
MAY	1 ♋ 27 ♌	1 ♓ 6 ♈	1 ♌	1 ♈ 24 ♉	1 ♌ 26 ♍	1 ♈ 3 ♉	1 ♍	1 ♉ 24 ♊	1 ♏ 6 ♎	1 ♉ 4 ♊
JUN	1 ♌	1 ♈ 15 ♉	1 ♌ 23 ♍	1 ♉	1 ♍	1 ♉ 12 ♊	1 ♍ 19 ♎	1 ♊	1 ♎	1 ♊ 16 ♋
JUL	1 ♌ 16 ♍	1 ♉ 27 ♊	1 ♍	1 ♉ 4 ♊	1 ♍ 21 ♎	1 ♊ 26 ♋	1 ♎	1 ♊ 6 ♋	1 ♎ 5 ♏	1 ♋
AUG	1 ♍	1 ♊	1 ♍ 12 ♎	1 ♊ 17 ♋	1 ♎	1 ♋	1 ♎ 14 ♏	1 ♋ 21 ♌	1 ♏	1 ♌
SEP	1 ♎	1 ♊ 12 ♋	1 ♎ 27 ♏	1 ♋	1 ♎ 7 ♏	1 ♋ 10 ♌	1 ♏ 29 ♐	1 ♌	1 ♏ 3 ♐	1 ♌ 17 ♍
OCT	1 ♎ 17 ♏	1 ♋	1 ♏	1 ♋ 5 ♌	1 ♏ 21 ♐	1 ♌ 30 ♍	1 ♐	1 ♌ 7 ♍	1 ♐ 17 ♑	1 ♍
NOV	1 ♏ 29 ♐	1 ♋	1 ♏ 9 ♐	1 ♌	1 ♐	1 ♍	1 ♐ 9 ♑	1 ♍ 27 ♎	1 ♑ 26 ♒	1 ♍ 4 ♎
DEC	1 ♐	1 ♋	1 ♐ 20 ♑	1 ♌ 12 ♍	1 ♑	1 ♍	1 ♑ 18 ♒	1 ♎	1 ♒	1 ♎ 23 ♏